C000043564

RAMUS
PUBLISHERS

As For Me And My House

We Will Serve The Lord
Joshua 24:15

Ricky Ramus
Author

This book was written with the intention of teaching and helping families overcome in their daily challenges at home.

The book then encourages those families to bring what they are doing at home to the church.

It was also written to inspire the churches to do what they are doing at church into their communities in a time where it is much needed.

When all the above has been done, I believe we will see God Bless our homes, our churches, and our communities, and belonging to the Christian family will always be treated as a privilege and a blessing.

I pray that this book blesses you and you enjoy reading it.

In Jesus Name. Amen.

1

DEDICATION

This book is dedicated to my brother
Pastor Lincoln Ramus

God have truly blessed me by placing him
as a Pastor over my life from the very beginning
of my ministry until this day.

He has watched and prayed for me
and always been there
even in very difficult times.

He has lived and set examples
of the teachings revealed in this book
and a legacy of testimonies.

I love you very much
and thank God from my heart
that I've been blessed to have you
as my brother and pastor.

Table of Contents

CHAPTER 1

The Son of Man is coming

Matthew 24:37-39
"But as the days of Noah were, so shall also the coming of the Son of man be. For as in the days that were before the flood they were eating and drinking, marrying and giving in marriage, until the day that Noah entered into the ark, And knew not until the flood came, and took them all away; so shall also the coming of the Son of man be."

The coming back of Christ is today compared with the days of Noah. I want you note that the main thing about Noah's story was the flood. Then main thing about the coming back of Christ will be the resurrection. I prefer to use the word resurrection instead of the word rapture as the word rapture is not mentioned in the Bible, but from the word resurrection we can clearly understand the Bible meaning.

St John 11:23-25
"Jesus saith unto her, Thy brother shall rise again. Martha saith unto him, I know that he shall rise again in the resurrection at the last day. Jesus said unto her, I am the resurrection, and the life: he that believeth in me, though he

were dead, yet shall he live:"

St John 14:1-3
"Let not your heart be troubled: ye believe in God, believe
also in me. In my Father's house are many mansions: if it
were not so, I would have told you. I go to prepare a place
for you. And if I go and prepare a place for you, I will come
again, and receive you unto myself; that where I am, there
ye may be also."

Jesus is definitely coming back and we can compare his
return to the flood of Noah.

I want you to note that after Noah's flood, all the unrighteous
people were carried away by the flood. After the
resurrection, at the coming back of Christ all the righteous
will be taken.

If all the people who perished in Noah's flood had a second
opportunity to change and be saved, I believe the majority
would have changed. They do not have that opportunity
whereas you and I have that opportunity today. When the
Son of Man comes back it will be too late just like Noah's
flood. This tells us that the most important period to be
saved was the time just before the flood, which I believe is
equivalent to the time we are living in today.

We must note that the times and events are compared to each other. I believe The Holy Spirit enlighten me that if we do what the righteous people did back then in Noah's time we will received the same reward and results today. We know that Noah and his family were saved. Let's look at what Noah did just before the flood.

Hebrews 11:7
"By faith Noah, being warned of God of things not seen as yet, moved with fear, prepared an ark to the saving of his house; by the which he condemned the world, and became heir of the righteousness which is by faith."

There is a lot of important information in this verse. I would like us to look at it very closely.

Hebrews 11:7
"By faith Noah, being warned of God of things not seen as yet,...."

Noah was warned by God. God spoke to Noah. Just like when God warned Noah and by faith Noah obeyed what God had told him, God is warning us today not only by the signs of the times, but through The Holy Spirit. The only way we are going to receive this warning is the same way Noah had done. Noah believed God and was moved inwardly. He was moved with fear by the images he had seen and his response was to the saving of his household.

Hebrews 11:7
"By faith Noah, being warned of God of things not seen as yet, moved with fear, prepared an ark to the saving of his house..."

Let's look at this closely to break it down very simply... (Paraphrasing)

God: "Noah! I'm sending a flood that no one has ever seen before."

Noah: "Are you sending a flood Lord?"

God: "Yes"

Noah: "I'm going to take care of my house."

God calls your name through the Holy Spirit and says "The Son of Man is coming and the righteous are going to be resurrected."

Us: "The Son of Man is coming Lord?"

God: "Yes"

What should our response be? Our response should be,

Us: "I'm going to take care of my house."

God is very concern about our house. He is concern about what is happening in our house, who is living in our house, who is coming to our house and the things we have in our house. God is very concerned about the activities and everything concerning our house.

Noah built the ark for the saving of his house. The ark was a place where God could dwell with Noah. It was the right environment for God's presence to be with Noah and his family. All men had become sinful and corrupted and sinful. The Bible tells us that there was no place for God to dwell on the earth in Noah's days. This was the reason why God decided to destroy the people by sending a flood.

The ark became a sanctuary between God and Man. We compare that time to today. God expects us to obey as Noah obeyed. God wants us to build Him a spiritual ark that he can also dwell with us and we can dwell in His presence.

Exodus 25:8-9
"And let them make me a sanctuary; that I may dwell among them. According to all that I shew thee, after the pattern of the tabernacle, and the pattern of all the instruments thereof, even so shall ye make it."

We will not become sons and daughters of God at the resurrection. The resurrection will be for those who are already the sons and daughters of God. These will be the people who have built a spiritual ark to save their house before the coming back of our Lord and Savior Jesus Christ. God is very concerned about our house.

Luke 11:17
"But he, knowing their thoughts, said unto them, Every kingdom divided against itself is brought to desolation; and a house divided against a house falleth."

Notice that Jesus said "...Every Kingdom divided against itself is brought to desolation..." He didn't say "...every church divided against itself..." but He said "...that a house divided against a house shall fall. You would think that the devil would be concentrating and attacking the church in these last days, but I want you to know that the church is too powerful for him. He cannot prevail against the church, so the only way he can be effective in bringing division into the church is to attack its members at home and let them bring their problems and bad habits to spread within the church. If the people of God can overcome at home, automatically when we come together as a church we will have the victory. IF WE CAN LEARN TO PRAY AT HOME, we will be able to pray effectively at church. IF WE CAN LEARN TO PRAISE AND

WORSHIP AT HOME, we will automatically know how too effectively have praise and worship at church. IF WE CAN LEARN TO LOVE AT HOME, WE WILL KNOW HOW TO LOVE AT CHURCH.

Hebrews 11:7
"By faith Noah, being warned of God of things not seen as yet, moved with fear, prepared an ark to the saving of his house; by the which he condemned the world,..."

I know that some of us Christians are worried and concerned about going out and witnessing to the world and we have many devices and plans on how to achieve this task, but the Word of God tells me that Noah whilst he took care of his house condemned the world. This shows us that by taking care of our house it will become an effective witness unto everyone who knows us. I want you to know that our correct actions at home will bring the presence of God on us so much that people will want to know more about our God and His loving grace. They will see for themselves that God is confirming every word that we speak.

Mark 16:20
"And they went forth, and preached every where, the Lord working with them, and confirming the word with signs following. Amen."

The revival that started in the book of "Acts of the Apostles" began from their houses. I strongly believe that God wants to release the same quality or greater revival. There will be a greater out pouring and these later days shall be greater than what was before, but we must understand that God's call has gone out and God is sending a special, fresh, greater outpouring of His Spirit for a much needed revival for today.

Hebrews 11:7
"By faith Noah, being warned of God of things not seen as yet, moved with fear, prepared an ark to the saving of his house; by the which he condemned the world, and became heir of the righteousness which is by faith."

I can boldly say that we will definitely become a hair of salvation and righteousness if we obey God's call and do what God wants us to do. Noah set an example to us. He was righteous with God which means right standing with God which also means he was in agreement with God and took the most import steps.....

God: "The Son of Man is coming?"

Us: "The son of Man is coming Lord? What shall I do?"

God: "Take care of your house!"

How do we make our House a sanctuary?

How do we build our Ark?

The answer to the above questions is:

☐ By doing what the entire Bible tells us to do

☐ By having church at church and church at home.

CHAPTER 2

The Church and Our Household

The church is a gathering of the body of Christ and we must be aware that when we come together it is a gathering of family.

Ephesians 2:19
"Now therefore ye are no more strangers and foreigners, but fellow citizens with the saints, and of the household of God;"

In chapter one Noah knew who himself and his family were. It is important that we understand the same thing as Noah. We must understand who we are and whom we belong too and who belongs to us. We must understand that we are fellow citizens with the saints and belong to the household of God. The function of the church is to establish this. When this is established we will find that the church becomes very effective and successful in its commission.

The teachings and activities that take place at church bring us victory within the church environment. It's is God's will not only for us to win at church, but also for us to win at home. To enable this to happen we need to implement the activities we do at church within our household environment. For us to build a spiritual ark so that God presence can be with us we must have church at home. God wants to use our churches as an example as to how Christians should overcome at home.

What does church mean?

The word "Church" comes from the Greek word "Ekklesia" which means "Called Out"

This is the understanding that we have been missing. We have been thinking that the church is a building or gathering of the saints, but the word simply means "Called Out".

God has called us out from amongst environments, from amongst people, from amongst friends, just like He had "Called Out" Noah. He has called us out for a purpose which will bring glory to His Name.

Jeremiah 1:5
"Before I formed thee in the belly I knew thee; and before thou camest forth out of the womb I sanctified thee, and I ordained thee a prophet unto the nations."

We are not only "Called Out" when we go to church, we are "Called Out" all the time. We have been called to fulfil God's purpose in our lifetime. We are "Called Out" even before we were formed in our mother's womb, sanctified and ordained in order to fulfil the purpose of God throughout our lives as well as in the lives of others.

Romans 8:29
"For whom he did foreknow, he also did predestinate to be conformed to the image of his Son, that he might be the firstborn among many brethren."

The activity that takes place when the church gathers together is meant to daily conform us into the image of Jesus Christ. This is why God wants us to have church at home.

To have church at home means that we are "Called Out" when we are at church and when we are at home. Our level of devotion should be the same when we are at church and when we are at home. Our level of worship should be the same when we are at church and when we are at home. Our level of prayer should be the same when we are at church and when we are at home. Our level of fellowship should be the same when we are at church and when we are at home. The family setting is the training ground that God uses to mold us into what He wants us to be.

What does it mean to have church at home?

It means doing in our home what we have been doing at church, such as prayer, exaltation, praise and worship and reading God's word in a family setting.

You may be thinking "I can't have church at home. My husband is not saved..." Well sinners come to your church, does that stop the service from taking place?

You may say "I can't have church at home because I live alone or haven't got a family..." You invite people to church, so you can invite friends or neighbours to have one hour devotion with you at home.

You may say "Well, it is just me and my children..." Well, you pray with the children at church, so you can pray with the children at home.

The biggest excuse that people use is "I haven't got enough time to spare..." What you are really saying is that you haven't got 30 minutes out of twenty four hours to spare for God each day and have fellowship and devotion with your family, but you have enough time to work, watch television, go on social media, and argue.

These are all deceptions used by the devil to stop people having church at home. Can you see what the devil is doing? Many people are finding the time to seek God as an individual, but not as a family. This is the reason why a lot of God's people are losing at home. If we have church at home every day, the power, security, protection and love that we feel when we are in His presence at church on weekends will also be felt every day of our lives. Why? Agreement and unity of our spirits is an important factor of winning at home. It must not be neglected. The devil understands that he is powerless when two or three Christians agree on a matter with unity in the spirit.

I want you to note that the activity that takes place within your church is done in agreement and unity of spirit. For an agreement to be made there must be two or more parties involved who are united in spirit. The reason for this is because God's power is released by agreement and unity in spirit.

Matthew 18:18-19
"Verily I say unto you, Whatsoever ye shall bind on earth shall be bound in heaven: and whatsoever ye shall loose on earth shall be loosed in heaven. Again I say unto you, That if two of you shall agree on earth as touching any thing that they shall ask, it shall be done for them of my Father which is in heaven."

People believe that this agreement is between one person and God. This is true, but the majority of cases there is more to it than just one person. The Word of God above says "...if two of you shall agree on earth ..." These words are written to highlight and emphasize on two physical human beings.

Ecclesiastes 4:9-12
"Two are better than one; because they have a good reward for their labour. For if they fall, the one will lift up his fellow:

but woe to him that is alone when he falleth; for he hath
not another to help him up. Again, if two lie together, then
they have heat: but how can one be warm alone? And if one
prevail against him, two shall withstand him; and a
threefold cord is not quickly broken."

The Bible verse above gives us the reason why two are better
than one. It also shows us that two persons will be able to
achieve more than one person. This is the reason why.
When two people come together in agreement and unity of
spirit they are able to withstand the devil. The cord is the
agreement whereby it changes from a twofold cord to a
threefold cord. That means instead of two parties involved,
there are now three parties involved.

God is a God of covenant. He is a God of agreement and
gives His covenant by using His Word. God must get involved
in order to bring that agreement to pass as promised in
Matthew 18:18-19, which says if two of you shall agree on
earth as touching anything they shall ask, it shall be done for
them.

Psalms 105:8
"He hath remembered his covenant for ever, the word
which he commanded to a thousand generations."

God made a covenant with Abraham and the blessings are
passed on to a thousand generations. He also made
promises to Jesus and those blessings are passed on to us.
God is a promise keeping, blessing sharing God.

Matthew 18:20

"For where two or three are gathered together in my name, there am I in the midst of them."

Another reason why it is very important for two people to come together is because of something I call "A Confession of Agreement."

What is a "Confession of Agreement?"

Romans 10:10

"For with the heart man believeth unto righteousness; and with the mouth confession is made unto salvation."

The Bible verse above says that "...confession is made unto salvation..." Confession of an agreement including God's word will automatically involve God. The word Salvation come from a a Greek word "Soteria" Soteria is the results of God Works. When we confess that God has worked on our behalf just like He promised, we will see the results of God's works in our lives. If we believe in our heart without doubt and confess what we believe, which is what God promised in His Word and establish that word in our heart, then we will receive God's salvation.

Isaiah 55:11
"So shall my word be that goeth forth out of my mouth: it shall not return unto me void, but it shall accomplish that which I please, and it shall prosper in the thing whereto I sent it."

When we combine agreement and God's word together, the word that describes the end result is "…accomplish…"

Matthew 18:16
"But if he will not hear thee, then take with thee one or two more, that in the mouth of two or three witnesses every word may be established."

Agreement + God's Word = Accomplished/Established

In order to have what we pray for we should seek someone to agree with our prayer. God will touch the right person's heart and get that person to pray a prayer of agreement quoting God's promise with us. We will then see the results of God's promises in our lives. "Soteria" which is known as "Salvation".

The power of God is released to work on our behalf only when we are in agreement. If we are divided, we have given the devil access to have power over us to stop the release of God's blessings in our lives.

Luke 11:17
"But he, knowing their thoughts, said unto them, Every kingdom divided against itself is brought to desolation; and a house divided against a house falleth."

CHAPTER 3

Having Church At Home

Joshua 24:15

"And if it seem evil unto you to serve the Lord, choose you
this day whom ye will serve; whether the gods which your
fathers served that were on the other side of the flood, or
the gods of the Amorites, in whose land ye dwell: but as for
me and my house, we will serve the Lord."

I believe the above statement that was made by Joshua
meant "Regardless of my environment and the people I am
with, I will have church at church and church at home."

The church is a place where we serve God. IT IS ALSO AN
EXTENSION OF THE FAMILY. The key facts are what we
do at church should also be done at home.

I want to point out to you from this book, the importance of
home fellowship and how much it can have an effect on our
church and on our community. My desire is to open your
understanding to the devises of the devil in our homes and
the success that will come from the Word of God when we
begin to have church at home.

Let us use the example where the household begins with a man and his wife.

Genesis 2:23-24
"And Adam said, This is now bone of my bones, and flesh of my flesh: she shall be called Woman, because she was taken out of Man. Therefore shall a man leave his father and his mother, and shall cleave unto his wife: and they shall be one flesh."

To have a change in our household the husband and wife must be in unity. If there is division this must be sorted out first then prayer should be done in unity.

Psalms 133:1-3
"Behold, how good and how pleasant it is for brethren to dwell together in unity! It is like the precious ointment upon the head, that ran down upon the beard, even Aaron's beard: that went down to the skirts of his garments; As the dew of Hermon, and as the dew that descended upon the mountains of Zion: for there the Lord commanded the blessing, even life for evermore."

The above verse says that when brethren dwell together in unity this can be compared to the dew that was upon the mountains of Hermon and Zion. The dew on Hermon and

Zion was plentiful even in dry weather. In the morning everything was wet as if it had rained. This descending dew can be compared to The Lord's presence dwelling with us.

We tend to look at the word "Brethren" as dealing with people in the church, but the surprising thing is that our wife is our brethren, our children are our brethren. Goodness comes from fellowship with husband and wife, goodness comes from fellowship with the children. That goodness is compared to the oil that ran down Aaron's the high priest beard even to the skirts of his garments. In the Bible oil is used as an expression of God's anointing power.

1 Samuel 16:13
"Then Samuel took the horn of oil, and anointed him in the midst of his brethren: and the Spirit of the Lord came upon David from that day forward. So Samuel rose up, and went to Ramah."

Isaiah 10:27
"And it shall come to pass in that day, that his burden shall be taken away from off thy shoulder, and his yoke from off thy neck, and the yoke shall be destroyed because of the anointing."

The anointing is the power of God to remove burdens and destroy yokes. I call it "...The burden removing, yoke destroying, power of God..." Oil is an expression of the anointing of the Holy Spirit. In the Bible we observe that people who have been set apart for the work of God are anointed with oil. This is symbolic of someone being anointed with The Holy Spirit today to prepare them for the work that God has pre-ordained them to complete. David was anointed as king by the prophet Samuel before he became king. When he was anointed with oil, the Spirit of God came upon him from that day onwards and helped him to become king.

God's word is letting us know that when two or more people such as husband and wife, mother and children, or the whole household come together in unity, the anointing will be poured out plentifully upon that household to remove their burdens and destroy their yokes bringing salvation to that household. That household will be fully furnished with blessings and the presence of God that will produce an atmosphere of love, peace, joy, long suffering, gentleness, goodness, faith, meekness and temperance. The fruit of our ground will come from the fruit of His Spirit and the blessings of The Lord will follow. There is also another important statement within this verse.

Psalms 133:3
"As the dew of Hermon, and as the dew that descended
upon the mountains of Zion: for there the Lord
commanded the blessing, even life for evermore."

The anointing is the channel which God has decided for His
Blessing to flow into our lives. It is important for households
to come together as a church in their own homes as brethren
come together in unity and have fellowship with God.

Psalms 133:1
"Behold, how good and how pleasant it is for brethren to
dwell together in unity! It is like the precious ointment upon
the head, that ran down upon the beard, even Aaron's
beard: that went down to the skirts of his garments;"

The devil's objective is to stop the unity within the
household. He is very subtle and cunning in the way he does
this and the devises he uses. One of the ways he does this is
by confusing each person's roll within the household
environment. Let us look at what the Bible says about the
rolls of a husband and wife. When we understand each
other's roles that God has given us, the unity in the
household is not easily broken.

Genesis 2:15,18

"And the Lord God took the man, and put him into the garden of Eden to dress it and to keep it.

And the Lord God said, It is not good that the man should be alone; I will make him an help meet for him."

Genesis 2:20-22

"And Adam gave names to all cattle, and to the fowl of the air, and to every beast of the field; but for Adam there was not found an help meet for him. And the Lord God caused a deep sleep to fall upon Adam, and he slept: and he took one of his ribs, and closed up the flesh instead thereof; And the rib, which the Lord God had taken from man, made he a woman, and brought her unto the man."

I want you to note that man was given position before he was given relationship. This explains why everything a man does is approached from a position point of view. It is always on the man's mind to excel in his job or increase what he can provide for his household as an expression of his love. This is different for a woman. Woman was given relationship first and they were created to help the man be the successful man God created him to be. This is why it is natural for a woman to always be looking for something she can help the man with. She obtains the same desire as God and believes that the man can be at his best and more successful when they do the task together and she is involved. Right here is where we identify what is needed to make a church successful and what will make the family home successful.

Position + Relationship

A man has the natural ability to quickly look at things as a whole with his attention to the outline of what the end result will be and what is needed to achieve it. A woman has the natural gift to pay attention to detail and the steps that are needed in order to achieve that end result. When they both use their natural gifts together, the rate of achieving success is increased and the journey will be more enjoyable and less stressful. They are both working together and both giving different expressions of love to God in the way that He desires to receive it. The problem arises in the household when roles and expressions are not understood clearly. When confusion sets into a relationship it allows the devil to cause great damage to our households.

Man was given position first and woman was given relationship. Man was given the commandment to look after the earth and woman was given the commandment to help him. It is through maximising our understanding of our position and relationship that will increase our success when we have church at church and church at home.

Noah ark had to be in a certain position and a certain relationship had to be established in that ark in order for his household to be saved.

CHAPTER 4

Understanding Our Position

The first thing that must be established in a household is to understand each other. The second is to use that understanding to communicate with each other.

It is very important for the head of that household to communicate with the rest of the members of that household and to constantly update them of the vision for that household. The devises of the devil is to breakdown that communication to cause confusion and division. The result of confusion and division will be disagreement in our household. If all the members of that household is not updated with the vision and progress that has been made they will not know what they should be helping with and if their efforts are contributing to achieving success for the household.

When we are at church, praise and worship refers to position and relationship. The teachings and ministering of the word refers to position and relationship. Our testimonies refer to position and relationship. Everything we do at church refers to both position and relationship and this should be our focal point in all our households.

What does the word "Position" mean?

The Bible word used for the word "Position" is "Place". The Greek word used for the word "Place" is "Topos" which means "Condition". When we are talking about our household position, we are really referring to our household condition.

Acts 2:1-3
"And when the day of Pentecost was fully come, they were all with one accord in one place. And suddenly there came a sound from heaven as of a rushing mighty wind, and it filled all the house where they were sitting. And there appeared unto them cloven tongues like as of fire, and it sat upon each of them."

I want us to note that before God is able to release His blessings in our lives, He requires a certain condition. The disciples were waiting to receive the baptism of The Holy Spirit, but they first had to be in one accord and also in the same condition. God requires a certain condition from our households. It's how we condition ourselves which will enable our blessing to get to us. The problems with most families is that they do not know what is that required condition.

We know that God requires certain conditions to be fulfilled by our household and only when those conditions are met by all the members within that household, only then will God fulfill His promises concerning our household and we will be blessed.

James 1:22
"But be ye doers of the word, and not hearers only, deceiving your own selves."

The above verse tells us to be doers of the word and not hearers only. It's how we position ourselves, which also means, how we condition ourselves, is the "doing" part of the word. The condition that God requires is not an outward one. People tend to think that God looks upon the big house, or the posh car, or the good job, but God's word tells me, "…deceiving your own selves…"Several times we deceive ourselves with the outward worldly things whereas God is a God who sees a man's heart and not looks at the outward appearance.

1 Samuel 16:7
"But the Lord said unto Samuel, Look not on his countenance, or on the height of his stature; because I have refused him: for the Lord seeth not as man seeth; for man looketh on the outward appearance, but the Lord looketh on the heart."

The condition that God is looking for is internal and not external. From the above verse we know that condition is located in the heart. This is not our physical heart; this is referring to the center of our existence, known as our spirit. We have a spirit and soul which lives in our body. Our spirit is also known as our heart. God does not look at the outward appearance of a person, but He looks at the heart, or we can say He looks at the spirit.

Proverb 4:23
"Keep thy heart with all diligence; for out of it are the issues of life."

What condition can be applied to the heart?

The only condition that can be applied to the heart is a believing condition, known also as a faith condition.

Hebrews 10:38
"Now the just shall live by faith: but if any man draw back, my soul shall have no pleasure in him."

How do we condition ourselves to live by faith?

To understand how to do this we must first understand how faith works. I will use the help of our five senses to explain.

We have five senses that have five different functions. Each sense has different purposes and responsibilities. These senses are;

1) See.   We use our Eyes to see.
2) Hear.   We use our ears to hear.
3) Taste. We use our mouth to taste.
4) Touch. We use our bodies to touch.
5) Smell. We use our nose to smell.

Each sense speaks to us and makes suggestions in order to influence our decision making. Together they all work in unity to enable the flesh (a person's body) to function in society. Let us look at each sense separately. From doing this we can truly understand how and why each sense will makes its own suggestions.

The eyes will only make a suggestion on what it sees. It will not take into consideration all the warning signals that comes from what we may touch, hear, taste, or smell. According to the eyes, everything that functions outside the seeing laws does not exist. It is the same with the nose, everything that functions outside the smelling laws does not exist. Repeatedly It is the same with the mouth and the rest of the body. Each one has its own existence and reality.

We have read that the just shall live by faith. To make faith easy to understand we will call it the sixth sense or "Faith Sense". This is the key! Now "Faith" has become a sense it is independent and will operate by itself and just like the other senses, it will not take into consideration the laws and suggestions of the other senses. The "Faith sense" works

33

independently from the other senses. What God wants from us is to live by the suggestion that comes from this sense, more than all the other senses we possess.

Now that we have acquired this knowledge, the question is;

How do we condition ourselves to live by faith?

The answer is;

We must choose to first come into agreement with everything that our faith sense is telling us.

This means we must bring all our other senses under the control of what our faith sense reveals to us.

I want us to note that we cannot see our senses, but every sense is housed in a physical part of us. Smelling is housed and associated with our nose. Seeing is housed and associated with our eyes. Hearing is housed and associated with our ears. Touching is housed and associated with our body. Tasting is housed and associated with our mouths. Where can we locate our "Faith sense" and what is it associated too?

Our "Faith sense" is housed and associated to The Word of God. Just like our ears, eyes, nose, mouth, and body are associated with us, the Bible is also associated to us. Although it may seem like it is separated from us and all the other senses, it is not. The reason why is because just like all the other senses are in us and is a part of us, our "Faith sense" is also in us and a part of us, which now tells me that The Word of God is also in us and a Part of us as well as being written and put in book form. When faith makes a suggestion to us, the only factors that it considers is The Word of God. The condition that God requires from us is to agree, submit and follow the suggestions given to us from our "Faith sense".

St John 15:7
"If ye abide in me, and my words abide in you, ye shall ask what ye will, and it shall be done unto you."

This is the process. Remember that the heart is our spirit. When we abide in the word of God, the word moves and travel into our spirit and connects with "The Word of God" that is already in our spirit, then our "Faith sense" will speak a suggestion to us concerning that word. Then whatever we ask in agreement to that suggestion will be granted unto us.

Matthew 12:34
"O generation of vipers, how can ye, being evil, speak good things? for out of the abundance of the heart the mouth speaketh."

Romans 10:17
"So then faith cometh by hearing, and hearing by the word of God."

When we speak that word out, we are releasing the faith condition required to bring that word to pass in our lives.

St John 1:14
"And the Word was made flesh, and dwelt among us, (and we beheld his glory, the glory as of the only begotten of the Father,) full of grace and truth."

Here is where we meet the condition that God wants us to meet. We must behold that word, believe that word, follow that word and most of all, and trust that word. Let us look at one example that accurately describes what I am trying to teach you, which is the example of Joshua and Caleb.

Numbers 13:1-2
"And the Lord spake unto Moses, saying, Send thou men, that they may search the land of Canaan, which I give unto the children of Israel: of every tribe of their fathers shall ye send a man, every one a ruler among them."

God promised the children of Israel the land of Canaan which was also known as the land flowing with milk and honey, the land of plenty. Before God gave them the land He wanted them to see it. He told them to send in spies before they could possess it.

Before God gives us anything He wants us to see it. He will tell us about it and then He will show it to us.

Numbers 13:17
"And Moses sent them to spy out the land of Canaan, and said unto them, Get you up this way southward, and go up into the mountain:"

Moses done what he was told and sent representatives to see the land.

We must be very careful concerning things that God and be mindful of what God wants us to see. Instead of coming back with what God wanted Moses' representatives to see, they saw something else and came back with what the Bible calls an evil report. There may be difficulties, problems, barriers and concerns surrounding what God will show us, but we must look and focus on the image that God shows us and trust Him for the details on how to overcome these things.

Numbers 13:25-33

"And they returned from searching of the land after forty days. And they went and came to Moses, and to Aaron, and to all the congregation of the children of Israel, unto the wilderness of Paran, to Kadesh; and brought back word unto them, and unto all the congregation, and shewed them the fruit of the land. And they told him, and said, We came unto the land whither thou sentest us, and surely it floweth with milk and honey; and this is the fruit of it. Nevertheless the people be strong that dwell in the land, and the cities are walled, and very great: and moreover we saw the children of Anak there. The Amalekites dwell in the land of the south: and the Hittites, and the Jebusites, and the Amorites, dwell in the mountains: and the Canaanites dwell by the sea, and by the coast of Jordan. And Caleb stilled the people before Moses, and said, Let us go up at once, and possess it; for we are well able to overcome it. But the men that went up with him said, We be not able to go up against the people; for they are stronger than we. And they brought up an evil report of the land which they had searched unto the children of Israel, saying, The land, through which we have gone to search it, is a land that eateth up the inhabitants thereof; and all the people that we saw in it are men of a great stature. And there we saw the giants, the sons of Anak, which come of the giants: and we were in our own sight as grasshoppers, and so we were in their sight."

Twelve men representing each tribe or we can say representing each family of Israel went to Canaan as spies. After forty days they came back with their own reports. They went to the same place. They experienced the same conditions, but when they returned they came back with two different reports. Ten of the representatives came back with what the Bible calls "…an evil report…" They said that they have seen everything that God has said about the land, nevertheless they also saw that the people who dwell in the land were big and strong giants and on seeing those giants they felt like grasshoppers in their own stature.

Why was it an evil report?

It was an evil report because they conditioned themselves wrongly to receiving the blessing that God had told them about. They saw and considered everything that their faith sense suggested to them, but also considered everything that their sight senses, touch sense, hear sense, smell sense and taste sense suggested to them. They did not put the other suggestions under control of what their Faith sense had suggested. By not doing this they gave birth to a "Nevertheless". The suggestions from our other senses will always bring another opinion known as a "Nevertheless". They will always give another outlook of what God has shown us. Why? The reason is because they do not consider the laws or conditions from the other senses. They abide under their own individual world's law and conditions. Another word for "Nevertheless" is "Doubt". Doubt can only come through the other senses which are not our "Faith sense". It can be strong enough to change what can be a good report into an evil report if we allow it. Why was it an evil report? It was an evil report because the devil has access to the flesh. All of our senses apart from our Faith sense are connected to our flesh. The devil has access to the flesh. We know the devil is a liar, which means he has access to those suggestions given to us by our senses. This means that he had the ability to lie to us and make us believe the lie which will then make us doubt what God has told us through our Faith sense (which is connected to His word) and make us give an evil report. This is why it is important for us to put all the other suggestions coming from our fleshly senses under control of what our Faith sense is suggesting to us. Those representatives broke the golden rule by not doing this by doubting their "Faith sense" which is where God's Word and Holy Spirit have influence. It is also the only sense where the devil has no access or no influence which means it's the only suggestion where he cannot lie to us.

Joshua and Caleb came back with a good report. They came back with what God wanted to show them.

Numbers 14:6-9
"And Joshua the son of Nun, and Caleb the son of Jephunneh, which were of them that searched the land, rent their clothes: And they spake unto all the company of the children of Israel, saying, The land, which we passed through to search it, is an exceeding good land. If the Lord

delight in us, then he will bring us into this land, and give it us; a land which floweth with milk and honey. Only rebel not ye against the Lord, neither fear ye the people of the land; for they are bread for us: their defence is departed from them, and the Lord is with us: fear them not."

The report of Joshua and Calib was founded upon what God had told them concerning the land of Canaan. What they saw and what they felt was based on what God had told them. They commanded every other sense to obey what their faith sense was telling them. They knew that everything that was in the land of Canaan belonged to them because God had spoken it and promised. This is what we should do today if we want to receive the same results.

The children of Israel chose to believe the report of the other ten spies over what Joshua and Calib told them. They chose not to believe their faith sense which meant they chose not to believe God.

Numbers 14:10-11
"But all the congregation bade stone them with stones. And the glory of the Lord appeared in the tabernacle of the congregation before all the children of Israel. And the Lord said unto Moses, How long will this people provoke me? and how long will it be ere they believe me, for all the signs which I have shewed among them?"

What was the end result?

Numbers 14:28-31

"Say unto them, As truly as I live, saith the Lord, as ye have spoken in mine ears, so will I do to you: Your carcases shall fall in this wilderness; and all that were numbered of you, according to your whole number, from twenty years old and upward, which have murmured against me, Doubtless ye shall not come into the land, concerning which I sware to make you dwell therein, save Caleb the son of Jephunneh, and Joshua the son of Nun. But your little ones, which ye said should be a prey, them will I bring in, and they shall know the land which ye have despised."

Everyone in our household should agree, obey and submit to their "Faith sense". We should put all other suggestions from the other senses under the control of our faith sense. This will enable us to meet God's required condition and we will be in the position to receive every blessing that God has for our household. If we chose to believe our other five senses over what God has promised, our end result will be like the children of Israel.

Are we ready to be in that position, that place, or that condition? To achieve this it takes maturity and maturity comes from something called "Relationship".

CHAPTER 5

Understanding Relationship

"...If we were to remove the Bible out of our lives we would be removing all possible contact with God..."

To understand this statement we need to look at the very first relationship that existed.

St John 1:1
"In the beginning was the Word, and the Word was with God, and the Word was God."

This verse refers to a "Beginning". The "Beginning" which this verse is referring to is concerning and centered on the beginning of the "Word".
In the beginning was the Word. The verse then states the position of the Word. (We have seen from the previous chapter that position is very important.)

The very important word here that explains everything is the word "with".

St John 1:1

The word "…with…" implies separation, but accompanying someone. "With" also implies that we are not that person, but we are beside or in the presence of that person. This means that the only way we can be "One" with that person is through relationship.

St John 1:2

"The same was in the beginning with God."

This verse is comparing the beginning of the Word with a process that happened before. The process of the Word was the same process of how the Holy Spirit began. How The Holy Spirit became separated from God, but still remains one with Him through relationship. I believe this is why in the New Testament; God is referred to as "Father". He is Father to the Holy Spirit and Father to the Word. The word became flesh and dwelled with us and because of the works of Jesus Christ we are now able to be sons and daughters of God, this also make Him Father to us.

1 John 5:7

"For there are three that bear record in heaven, the Father, the Word, and the Holy Ghost: and these three are one."

God separated Himself into three dimensions. He did this for us to have the power and influence that is released through relationship. We must truly understand that our position and condition can be strengthened by our relationship. Let us look at another example, the beginning of man.

Genesis 1:26-27
"And God said, Let us make man in our image, after our likeness: and let them have dominion over the fish of the sea, and over the fowl of the air, and over the cattle, and over all the earth, and over every creeping thing that creepeth upon the earth. So God created man in his own image, in the image of God created he him; male and female created he them."

Genesis 2:7
"And the Lord God formed man of the dust of the ground, and breathed into his nostrils the breath of life; and man became a living soul."

God created man male and female. When God created Adam who was male, He also created the female inside of Adam. Eve and Adam was "Man". They were "one" in the beginning. God crated man in His own image. He created Eve (Woman) out of from the bone and flesh of Man. Eve was created and formed from inside of Adam then separated. Man and woman were one in the beginning then God separated the woman from inside that man and they then became "One" through relationship.

How do I know this?

When God decided to bring forth Eve (the female) He did not make her with the materials from the ground. He made her with the materials from inside Adam (the male).

Why did God do this?

God did this because male and female must still remain "One" through "Relationship" after they became separated, just like God and His Word are "One".

Genesis 2:21-22
"And the Lord God caused a deep sleep to fall upon Adam, and he slept: and he took one of his ribs, and closed up the flesh instead thereof; And the rib, which the Lord God had taken from man, made he a woman, and brought her unto the man."

After God made Eve the position and condition of man was stronger than it had ever been before. Although the female was now separated from the male, through relationship they both were able to do things and achieve much more. Why do I state this? The reason is before God made the separation between male and female, He made the following statement.

Genesis 2:18
"And the Lord God said, It is not good that the man should be alone; I will make him an help meet for him."

After the female was with the male they remained one through relationship. Man's (male and female) character needed to be formed and developed. In order for this to be correctly done just like God wanted, it had to be done through relationship. The purpose of why God created man could not be fulfilled if they remained as one.

Genesis 2:23-24
"And Adam said, This is now bone of my bones, and flesh of my flesh: she shall be called Woman, because she was taken out of Man. Therefore shall a man leave his father and his mother, and shall cleave unto his wife: and they shall be one flesh."

I remember the summer of 1999 when I believed the Lord spoke the following words to me through the Holy Spirit.

"Everything about Me is three dimensional"
"Everything about you is three dimensional"
"Our relationship is three dimensional"

There three sentences kept on repeating itself to me through my "Faith Sense". I felt it gain victory in my spirit, because I had received it as a good report and put all my other senses suggestions under the control of these three sentences. I felt it gain victory in my soul and body too. It changed the way I saw and did things at that time and I began to see the blessings that God had promised me manifest in my life. It was revealed to me that at that time God wanted me to see everything to do with relationship three dimensionally. The activities that we did at church must be done three dimensionally. Praise and worship, prayer, preaching, teaching, exaltations and testimonies must be done three dimensionally. Everything we participated in at church or at home should be done three dimensionally in order for us to have success, victory and revival that the word of God wanted us to receive.

What does "Three Dimensional" mean?

The word "Dimension" in the Webster's dictionary means "Measurement of extension (as in length, height, or breadth). These measurements are mentioned in the Bible in the following verse.

Ephesians 3:17-19

"That Christ may dwell in your hearts by faith; that ye, being rooted and grounded in love, May be able to comprehend with all saints what is the breadth, and length, and depth, and height; And to know the love of Christ, which passeth knowledge, that ye might be filled with all the fulness of God."

The above verse is talking about "…being filled with all the fullness of God…" through His three dimensional love.

This verse could also be interpreted to say "…may be able to comprehend with all the saints what is three dimensional and to know the love of Christ, which passeth knowledge and understanding , that ye might be filled with the fullness of God. " Love is the most powerful influence in the heavens and the earth. It ability to be released totally relies on relationship.

Let us put it all together and look back on the three sentences the Lord Jesus spoke to me through The Holy Spirit.

"Everything about Me is three dimensional"
"Everything about you is three dimensional"
"Our relationship is three dimensional"

Remember the word "Dimension" means "measurement of extension", also Ephesians 3:18 talks about God's love. What God was saying to me was;

"Everything about Me is extended love"
"Everything about you is extended love"
"Our relationship is extended love"

We must note that God is three dimensional. This means that everything about God is extended love. Love is only expressed through relationship. This is the reason why God made man in His own image.

Genesis 1:26-27
"And God said, Let us make man in our image, after our likeness: and let them have dominion over the fish of the sea, and over the fowl of the air, and over the cattle, and over all the earth, and over every creeping thing that creepeth upon the earth. So God created man in his own image, in the image of God created he him; male and female created he them."

This verse shows us that God is three dimensional. Man is also three dimensional. He has a spirit, soul and a body. Therefore when a man receives the gospel of Jesus Christ into his heart (spirit), he receives the three dimensions of God (The Father, The Word, The Holy Spirit) in his spirit.

Romans 8:9-11

"But ye are not in the flesh, but in the Spirit, if so be that the Spirit of God dwell in you. Now if any man have not the Spirit of Christ, he is none of his. And if Christ be in you, the body is dead because of sin; but the Spirit is life because of righteousness. But if the Spirit of him that raised up Jesus from the dead dwell in you, he that raised up Christ from the dead shall also quicken your mortal bodies by his Spirit that dwelleth in you."

The nature of God is in us. The Father sent His word and Holy Spirit to dwell inside of man. These two represent The Father and preforms a three dimensional work. The three dimensional work is known as "A work of extended love." We can have a true, good and successful relationship with each other when we allow God's love to function in our spirit. That love which is in our spirit, is passed through our souls and bodies, gaining victory over all circumstances by God's Word. God sent His word into man to effect the three areas in man's existence, our spirit, our soul, and our body.

Isaiah 55:11

"So shall my word be that goeth forth out of my mouth: it shall not return unto me void, but it shall accomplish that which I please, and it shall prosper in the thing whereto I sent it."

God is talking about an accomplished finished word that brings prosperity. He speaks that word into man's spirit which means man become prosperous in his spirit, but the word is not completed until it passes through the other two dimensions bringing prosperity also in his soul and body. This can be achieved because;

1. There is a relationship between your spirit, your soul and your body.
2. The word is the vehicle for The Father, The Word and The Holy Spirit.

Whatever area (spirit, soul, or body) we receive God's word; He will be able to extend His love to us through relationship. This is where our supply will come from for all our need. We must receive God's Word totally in our sprit, soul and body in order for His word to be complete in our lives.

I will never forget the difference the extension made on that house. It transformed the house to another class. It looked different in breadth, length, depth and height. The extension became part of the house and it made the house larger in size, functions and capabilities. When the extension started it was an addition to the house, but when it was finished it became a part of the house.

God's intention is to extend His love towards us in breadth, length, depth and height. God is building an extension just like that house. When that extension is finished, the part of us where that extension has been built will be even more beautiful than it was before and we will increase in our capabilities. Our appearance will be better and we will become a better person. Our value will also increase. People will be drawn to stop, look and talk about the glory of God that is on our lives.

God's extension will make a big difference. It will release favour into our lives.

God builds love in our heart (spirit). He then extends it to our soul and body. At the end of the process we become a product of love. Everything we do will be done from the root of love. Everything we say will be form the root of love. Everything about us will be extended love, just like everything about Him is extended love.

Ephesians 2:4

"But God, who is rich in mercy, for his great love wherewith he loved us,"

1 John 4:16

"And we have known and believed the love that God hath to us. God is love; and he that dwelleth in love dwelleth in God, and God in him."

When the Lord told me to write this chapter I began to try and research relationships between humans. The Holy Spirit revealed to me that I could not generalise love. Everybody is different and has different needs, they live in different environments and have different circumstances. I prayed and asked God "How Can I teach your people to have a successful relationship at home?" He said "Teach them about how to have a romantic relationship with me and I will teach them how to have a romantic relationship with each other.

1 Thessalonians 4:9

"But as touching brotherly love ye need not that I write unto you: for ye yourselves are taught of God to love one another."

The Bible teaches us that God is love. This is a special type of love called "Agape Love". God's love is "Agape Love". We must understand that God's love is expressed through His actions. If we carefully look at the actions of The Father, The Word, and the Holy Spirit towards each other, we will see that it serves as an example of how we should treat each other in our relationship.

What is the relationship between The Father, The Word, and The Holy Spirit?

1. The Father

God is known as The Father because He is the source where everything was created. The Hebrew word used for God is "Elhoim" which means "The Creator". The Greek word used for "Father" is "Abba" which means "The Source". Everything that was created started from inside "The Father". "The Father" released all things outside of Him by "The Word".

2. The Word

The Word of God takes what was in The Father and transform it into man's environment.

3. The Holy Spirit

The Holy Spirit Is the part of God that brings the manifestation of what was released out of "The Father" through the vehicle of "The Word".

Isaiah 34:16
"Seek ye out of the book of the Lord, and read: no one
of these shall fail, none shall want her mate: for my
mouth it hath commanded, and his spirit it hath
gathered them."

Whatever God creates into existence then becomes an
expression of love and an extension of love because it
returns to its creator.

We have seen that the word "God" means "Creator".
We have also seen the process of how creation was
made. Now if we look at how "The Father", "The Word",
and "The Holy Spirit" work together, this will be a good
example of how we should work together and receive
successful results.

- ☐ Person.
- ☐ Personality.
- ☐ Character.

If we put the above together we are talking about one
person with three parts to Himself.

- ☐ "The Word" is the personality of "The Father".

"The Word" speaks for "The Father". He is the communicator, interpreter and expression of everything that The Father is and wants to create.

- [ ] "The Holy Spirit" is the personality of "The Word" and also the character of "The Father".

"The Holy Spirit" administrates for "The Word". He brings manifestation to what has been spoken into existence.

How does all this affect us?

We are spirit beings and we are connected to God through His personality and His character. (The Word and The Holy Spirit) We must live our lives to be the personality of The Holy Spirit and The Character of The Word in order to extend God's love.

- [ ] The personality of The Holy Spirit is the anointing.
- [ ] The character of The Word is, doing good, i.e. To heal the broken hearted. To preach deliverance to the captives. The recovering of sight to the blind. Set liberty to them that is bruised. To preach the acceptable year of The Lord. Heal all that is oppressed by the devil.

Acts 10:38

"How God anointed Jesus of Nazareth with the Holy Ghost
and with power: who went about doing good, and healing
all that were oppressed of the devil; for God was with him."

Whenever the Bible talks about God doing anything for His
people we must know that it is an act of love. When we read
about healing, deliverance and blessings etc. They are all
expressions of God's love for his people. Receiving the
Baptism of The Holy Spirit is also an expression of God's love.
When we examine all the things that God has done for us we
will truly see how much God loves us. When someone shows
an expression of his or her love towards each other it is
known as "Romance". When I look at God's actions in
my life, I can truly say "God loves me and is very romantic
towards me." Jesus Christ was the true expression of God's love
for His people when He walked on this earth as man. God's
intention is for His love to be extended into our homes in order
to strengthen our position in life.

Ephesians 5:25

"Husbands, love your wives, even as Christ also loved
the church, and gave himself for it;"

The above comparison tells us that we must know the way
Christ loved the church before we can truly love our wives

the way God wants us too. The Church is compared to the bride. God expects the husband to have the same love for their wives. The way to release love in our relationship is by knowing our partners. When I did a survey about relationships I found that the majority of information people knew about each other was revealed during their time of being romantic to each other. They found out each other's likes and dislikes, what each other prefers to wear and eat, the type of films, series and programs they both like to watch, and the type of house and cars they both like. All this was revealed through communication during time of romance. It is the same way with God. Our God is a romantic God. When we get a revelation from God, this means that God is allowing us to know more about Him so He can release His Extended love to us. I want us to fully understand that our reading, prayer, meditation and worship times are romantic moments. God is getting to know us and allowing us to know more about Him. His love is then expressed by the things he will do for us because of those romantic moments shared together with Him.

Everything we do to please God such as prayer, worship, praise, meditation, reading His word is a romantic gesture towards Him. We do this to know more about Him. In return, everything God does for us such as forgiveness, provision, healing, protection, is an expression and extension of His love towards us. The more experienced we are at doing the above romantic gestures will provide us with more manifestation and expression of God's love in our lives. This is the reason why it is important we must do these things not only in our church environment but also in our household environment. The more often we do these activities, the better we will become at doing them. There will always be more opportunities in our home environment to do these things more than the opportunity of doing them when we all come together at church. It is the will of God that we become skilled at the above as a family before we are able to fulfil our purpose effectively for what we were created to achieve.

In order to have 100% victory over the devil in our homes, in order to prepare for the coming of The Son of Man and the resurrection, we must allow God's love and presence to flow throughout our household.

- "Relationship" is God's Bible school.
- The theology of relationship can only be taught by God.
- Relationship was made only for the expression and advancement of love.

A house with a good relationship is a house full of love.

Let us put it all together and understand why God is concerned about our household and family lives.

CHAPTER 7

From A Family to a Nation

We must understand that God has chosen us and placed
what is known as a "Calling" which means "Purpose" on our
lives. From our household He will build Himself a nation for
His Name.

Acts 15:14
"Simon hath declared how God at the first did visit the
Gentiles, to take out of them a people for his name."

We must realise that we are a part of that chosen generation
who God has called out to be a part of His "Holy Nation".
God out of His love visited our ancestors when they were
known as "Gentiles" to take out of them people for His
"Holy Nation".

Because of what God did back then we are now a part of that
"Holy Nation" today.

1 Peter 2:9
"But ye are a chosen generation, a royal priesthood, an holy
nation, a peculiar people; that ye should shew forth the praises of
him who hath called you out of darkness into his marvellous
light:"

The verse above tells us who we are and what we should be doing. We have been called out of darkness (sin) into His marvellous light (righteousness). We were not accepted, but now we are accepted. By God's mercy we were not God's people, but are now God's People.

Why did God do this?

God has done this to make us part of His Holy Nation. The activities we do as a family member to maintain our household is what God wants us to do when we go to war as His "Holy Nation". God wants us to show forth what we learnt in our training. He wants us to skilfully use how we conditioned ourselves and maintain relationship as part of His "Holy Nation" when we go to war. These principles are a part of God's statutes and judgements.

Deuteronomy 4:5-6
"Behold, I have taught you statutes and judgments, even as the Lord my God commanded me, that ye should do so in the land whither ye go to possess it. Keep therefore and do them; for this is your wisdom and your understanding in the sight of the nations, which shall hear all these statutes, and say, Surely this great nation is a wise and understanding people."

The verse above says that we must keep them and do them. Praise, worship, teaching, preaching, prayer and meditation in God's word together as a household is keeping His statutes and judgements. Having a romantic time with God is a very good reason to keeping His statutes and judgements. Having church at home is the training needed to keeping His statutes and judgements. The outcome of doing this is;

- ☐ We will be a part of God's "Holy Nation".
- ☐ We will be looked upon as a wise and understanding people.

Deuteronomy 4:7
"For what nation is there so great, who hath God so nigh unto them, as the Lord our God is in all things that we call upon him for?"

What makes us great is that we have God near to us. Having church at home, having those romantic times, our prayer, worship and meditating times are done, so we can have God near to us and by putting all our senses under the control of our "Faith Sense",

Ephesians 2:4-7
"But God, who is rich in mercy, for his great love wherewith he loved us, Even when we were dead in sins, hath quickened us together with Christ, (by grace ye are saved;) And hath raised us up together, and made us sit together in heavenly places in Christ Jesus: That in the ages to come he

might shew the exceeding riches of his grace in his kindness toward us through Christ Jesus."

To be a part of God's Holy Nation we must have nearness to God. That nearness for us comes by Jesus Christ through the Holy Spirit. Remember they are the expression of God's Personality and God's Character and through them God is able to express His extended love to us.

Deuteronomy 4:8
"And what nation is there so great, that hath statutes and judgements so righteous as all this law, which I set before you this day?"

We must value our time that we have spent with God. We must value His status and judgements that we have learnt during our time with Him. They will give us wisdom and understanding. They will enable us to see things the way God want us to see them, so we will comeback with a good report. They will give us instruction on what we should do to take the land God promised us.

Romans 8:18

"For I reckon that the sufferings of this present time are not worthy to be compared with the glory which shall be revealed in us."

The above verse informs us that there is a glory which shall be revealed in us greatly exceeds the sufferings that we are experiencing and seeing today. It says that there can be no comparison between the two. The reason why is because "The Holy Spirit" expresses the personality of "The Word" and we express the character of "The Holy Spirit".

Deuteronomy 4:9

"Only take heed to thyself, and keep thy soul diligently, lest thou forget the things which thine eyes have seen, and lest they depart from thy heart all the days of thy life: but teach them thy sons, and thy sons' sons;"

By doing what the above verse says, we will never forget that God is always extending His love towards us and then we become the expression of His love to others.

Before we can become part of God's "Holy Nation" ready for war, we must have gone through family training. In the time that we are living in today, before we can make a effective change within our community when should of went through training on how to position ourselves correctly and how to release the strength and power that comes from relationship and unity.

1 Corinthians 13:11
"When I was a child, I spake as a child, I understood as a child, I thought as a child: but when I became a man, I put away childish things."

Paul said, when he was a child he thought as a child, but now that he is a man he put away childish things. It takes a trained male or female to fight against other Nations that will come up against God's "Holy Nation". It will be what we have learnt and the training that we have been through as a spiritual child, that will determine how matured and skilful we will be for God purpose when called upon and required. God brought His statutes and judgement out of Himself and placed them into our spirit, so that we can bring His status and judgement out of us into our environment.

1 Samuel 17:32-37
"And David said to Saul, Let no man's heart fail because of him; thy servant will go and fight with this Philistine. And Saul said to David, Thou art not able to go against this Philistine to fight with him: for thou art but a youth, and he a man of war from his youth. And David said unto Saul, Thy

servant kept his father's sheep, and there came a lion, and a bear, and took a lamb out of the flock: And I went out after him, and smote him, and delivered it out of his mouth: and when he arose against me, I caught him by his beard, and smote him, and slew him. Thy servant slew both the lion and the bear: and this uncircumcised Philistine shall be as one of them, seeing he hath defied the armies of the living God. David said moreover, The Lord that delivered me out of the paw of the lion, and out of the paw of the bear, he will deliver me out of the hand of this Philistine. And Saul said unto David, Go, and the Lord be with thee."

Another example we can refer to is David. David faced the lion and the bear before he went to war against Goliath. The lion and bear was his training ground. How do I know? Because David drew reference to how he defeated the lion and bear when he sleighed Goliath. In our family setting we are facing the lion and bear. As we learn how to deal with them, God is imputing into our spirits, war tactics, war methods, war gifts, and as we fight we are getting war training. If David did not war against the lion and bear he would not have been able to defeat Goliath. He was a family boy tending the sheep. He became a soldier for God's army. Having church at home will get us ready to be a soldier for God's army and when soldiers came together in the Bible they became a nation ready for war.

Judges 3:1-2

"Now these are the nations which the Lord left, to prove
Israel by them, even as many of Israel as had not known all
the wars of Canaan; Only that the generations of the
children of Israel might know, to teach them war, at the
least such as before knew nothing thereof;"

The verse above states that God left that nation on purpose.
He could have wiped them out and got rid of them. He chose
not to wipe them out of existence before because He wanted
to prove Israel by them. Some of the problems and
challenges we are facing in our lives today are because God
wants to prove us by them like He did with the children of
Israel. God left them there. He could have removed them
and got rid of them. He allowed them to happen and
purposely left them there so that He can prove us by them.
He wants to prove us to whatever and whoever needs to see
and hear our testimony of how we overcame whether it be
other nations, what the Bible calls principalities and powers
and spiritual wickedness, sickness or any challenges we must
face. We are part of His army; we are a part of His "Holy
Nation". We have God close to us and we are skilfully
trained. No weapons that are formed against us shall
prosper. Our challenges are in our lives because God wants
to prove [Say your name] and teach [Say your name] war.
He has left some things in our lives so He can teach us how to
overcome them. He has left some things in our lives to teach

us how to position ourselves by His love that is released through relationship. I remember a preacher once said "If I didn't have any problems, I would have not known that God could solve them."

Ephesians 6:12
"For we wrestle not against flesh and blood, but against principalities, against powers, against the rulers of the darkness of this world, against spiritual wickedness in high places."

Matthew 11:12
"And from the days of John the Baptist until now the kingdom of heaven suffereth violence, and the violent take it by force."

For we fight not against flesh and blood, but against principalities and powers of darkness and spiritual wickedness in heavenly places. The Kingdom of Heaven suffered violence and the violence takes it by force. This is why we must have church at home. This is why we must become skilled in having fellowship with God. This is why it's important to enjoy our romantic moments and get to know God more. These are our lion and bear moments and are very needful. There is going to come a time in our lives that we need to be ready to meet our Goliath and also be able to defeat him. God has left the "Other Nations" in our lives to war against them. Spiritually speaking, these "Other Nations" are the challenges we face. We are expected to war against these spiritual powers and challenges, and not war physically against the people who are utilised and are controlled by the devil and his forces. Those people we leave in God's hands to deal with.

Romans 12:19
"Dearly beloved, avenge not yourselves, but rather give place unto wrath: for it is written, Vengeance is mine; I will repay, saith the Lord."

How do we overcome our problems and challenges?

Judges 3:4
"And they were to prove Israel by them, to know whether they would hearken unto the commandments of the Lord, which he commanded their fathers by the hand of Moses."

We overcome our problems and challenges by what we have learned in training.
- How to position (condition) ourselves by our relationship with God.

☐ How to improve our relationship with God and what we know about Him with romantic gestures such as praise, worship, prayer, and meditation on God's word.

This will move God into extending His love towards us so we can express that love to others. This expression of God's love is known as His "Anointing".

What is God's Anointing?

Isaiah 10:27
"And it shall come to pass in that day, that his burden shall be taken away from off thy shoulder, and his yoke from off thy neck, and the yoke shall be destroyed because of the anointing."

The anointing is the power of God that is able to remove burdens that weighs His people down and destroy yokes that are choking His people's necks. It is known as "The Burden Removing, Yoke Destroying, Power of God".

What should the anointing be used for?

Act 10:38

"How God anointed Jesus of Nazareth with the Holy Ghost
and with power: who went about doing good, and healing
all that were oppressed of the devil; for God was with him."

It should only be used to do good by healing and stoping all
oppression of the devil.

God saved a poor and scared family out of Egypt but it was a
fully trained nation that went and fought against the
Amalekites. It was the training that they received as a family
that made them into a "Holy Nation".

The anointing that comes from the Holy Spirit, was given to
Jesus the Christ. Jesus was the Anointed One. Jesus
went around using that power to heal all that was oppressed
of the devil and also for doing good wherever He went. We
are now expected to use that very same anointing, now that
we have access to it and that anointing must be used for the same
reasons, with us expecting to see the same results and the same
demonstration of power.

CHAPTER 8

Fighting As a Nation

When God delivered Israel out of Egypt they were a family but by the time they had their first battle against the Amalekites they were a Nation. It's time for us to have our first battle as part of God's Holy Nation. We must treat the problems and challenges we are going through as the Amalekites in order to overcome them. At the beginning of this book we were part of a family and the main focus was on our household. Now that is has been revealed that when we were concentrating and focusing on our households and families, there was is a bigger picture. The bigger picture is that God was training us to be a part of His Holy Nation. We are now encountering the Amalekites in our lives. We must use all that we have learnt to overcome them and win this battle. The key thing about fighting as a Nation is to fight "Together". We must fight as a unit and not as individuals. We must use the skills we have learnt about position, condition, and relationship. Let us highlight what we should have learnt in our training as part of a Nation.

The following testimony about how Israel as a Nation overcame the Amalekites highlights some important points.

Exodus 17:8
"Then came Amalek, and fought with Israel in Rephidim."

Amalek was a nation and the Amalekites were the people of Amalek. They did not have a covenant with God and stood for everything that was against God. Our problems will eventually attack us just like the Amalekites attacked Israel. This is because we have a covenant with God through Jesus Christ. We should be prepared and ready. We should always remember that we are part of a Holy Nation just like Israel did and we should always remember that God is on OUR side. We must see what God see and come back with a good report and not an evil one. God will make sure we will win the battle as long as we are trained and prepared for it.

Exodus 17:9
"And Moses said unto Joshua, Choose us out men, and go out, fight with Amalek: tomorrow I will stand on the top of the hill with the rod of God in mine hand."

When we are fighting as a Nation it means that we are fighting together. It means that the well trained members of the church are going to war to fulfil its purpose and vision. Moses said "Choose us out men, and go out, fight with Amalekites." What Moses meant was "Choose the men who are ready to fight. Choose the men who remember their training."

Ephesians 6:12
"For we wrestle not against flesh and blood, but against principalities, against powers, against the rulers of the darkness of this world, against spiritual wickedness in high places."

Behind every one of our problems is one of these active forces. These forces are our Amalekites and we must be ready to fight against them.

"Choose us out men (male of female), and go out, fight with Amalekites."

"Choose some men (male or female) who skilfully know how to pray together as a unit. That knows how to worship together as a unit. That knows how to apply the word of God together as a unit in warfare."

"Choose men (male or female) who are willing to trust the word of God with their lives because they understand God's love."

"Choose us out men (male or female) who know how to position themselves and also understand that their relationship with God and their relationship with each other is the strength of their position."

Some of the men with Moses were not ready for this battle. The reason why I know this is because Moses said to Joshua the words "Choose some men...." Some of the men were not ready for battle.

Just having training at church is not enough to make us skilful to fight this battle. We need to remember what we did when we faced our lion and bear. It's very important that we remember the training we received as a family. Why? Our mentality will change from thinking like a family to thinking as a Nation. Thinking as a Nation can only come by experiencing our family training. It's the next required level. Our mentality is very important. The way we think will have an effect on the way we perform.

Proverbs 23:7
"For as he thinketh in his heart, so is he: Eat and drink, saith he to thee; but his heart is not with thee."

2 Corinthians 10:3-6

"For though we walk in the flesh, we do not war after the
flesh: (For the weapons of our warfare are not carnal, but
mighty through God to the pulling down of strong holds;)
Casting down imaginations, and every high thing that
exalteth itself against the knowledge of God, and bringing
into captivity every thought to the obedience of Christ; And
having in a readiness to revenge all disobedience, when
your obedience is fulfilled."

We must note the following:

- ☐ Our spiritual weapons of warfare are mighty enough
  to pull down strongholds.
- ☐ Our spiritual weapons are able to cast down
  imaginations.
- ☐ Our spiritual weapons are powerful enough to
  capture every thought to the obedience of Christ.

Exodus 17:10

"So Joshua did as Moses had said to him, and fought with
Amalek: and Moses, Aaron, and Hur went up to the top of
the hill."

Moses went to the top of the hill to make intercession (Pray) for Israel. Jesus is doing the same thing for us today. Jesus intercedes for us with "The Father" as we fight our battle with the Amalekites.

Romans 8:34
"Who is he that condemneth? It is Christ that died, yea rather, that is risen again, who is even at the right hand of God, who also maketh intercession for us."

We need someone on top of the hill for us today. Jesus Christ has risen again to take up that position for us. We have a better person than Moses on top of the hill making intercession for us. This means that we can expect even better results from our battles.

When Moses went up to the top of the hill he did not go alone. He took two more people with him. He took Aaron and Hur with him. Here is another important point of reference. To win a battle it is going to take the prayer of agreement and unity.

Matthew 18:19
"Again I say unto you, That if two of you shall agree on earth as touching anything that they shall ask, it shall be done for them of my Father which is in heaven."

Jesus requires the same action from us today. He has given us a system whereby "The Father", "Jesus the Word" and "The Holy Spirit" are one through relationship, are on top of the hill making intercession and doing what is required for us to win the battle in our lives. We must also do the same thing at the bottom of the hill. We must do our part and what is required of us in this battle. We must fight together in unity as a Nation knowing that we have support and access to what is happening on top of the hill.

Ephesians 2:6
"And hath raised us up together, and made us sit together in heavenly places in Christ Jesus:"

Exodus 17:11-13
"And it came to pass, when Moses held up his hand, that Israel prevailed: and when he let down his hand, Amalek prevailed. But Moses' hands were heavy; and they took a stone, and put it under him, and he sat thereon; and Aaron and Hur stayed up his hands, the one on the one side, and the other on the other side; and his hands were steady until the going down of the sun. And Joshua discomfited Amalek and his people with the edge of the sword."

Moses was on top of the hill with Aaron and Hur praying while the Israelites were at the bottom of the hill fighting against the Amalekites. When Moses lifted up his hands Israel were winning the battle, but when his hands went down Israel were losing the battle. They put Moses to sit on a stone. Another word used for stone is "Rock". They put Moses to sit on a "Rock" and they held his hands up until Israel prevailed and won the battle.

Matthew 16:15-18
"He saith unto them, But whom say ye that I am? And Simon Peter answered and said, Thou art the Christ, the Son of the living God. And Jesus answered and said unto him, Blessed art thou, Simon Bar–jona: for flesh and blood hath not revealed it unto thee, but my Father which is in heaven. And I say also unto thee, That thou art Peter, and upon this rock I will build my church; and the gates of hell shall not prevail against it."

Jesus asked Simon;
 "But whom say ye that I am?"
- ☐ This is a very important question. I want us to truthfully answer that question ourselves and listen to our own answer. Simon Peter answered
"Thou art the Christ, the son of the living God."
- ☐ Was our answer the same or different to Simon Peter? If it was not, we are not ready for battle and we need more training. If it was not the same we will

not be chosen with the men that will go to fight as
part of that "Holy Nation."

If our answer was the same as Simon Peter, it
informs us that we are nearly there with one more
condition to be met.

"Blessed art thou, Simon Barjona: for flesh and blood hath
not revealed it unto thee, but my Father which is in heaven."

- ☐ The source of our answer is very important. Our
  answer is not good enough or strong enough to
  release the "Blessing" this verse is talking about if it
  came from hearing it from someone else (flesh and
  blood). God will use someone else to confirm what
  He has told you to release the power that comes
  from agreement.

  That power required to win this battle comes from;
    - o Knowing the source where this information
      came from.
    - o Knowing that important information came
      from "The Father" which is in heaven.

If these conditions are met we are ready. If we know
what it means that Jesus is the Christ and He is the
son of the living God and that He is now on top of the
hill making intersession for us and everything that we
know and believe concerning this topic was revealed
to us by "Abba Father" which art in heaven and we
are rooted and grounded in believing this knowledge,

then we are truly ready to be a part of God's chosen Nation ready for battle.

"And I say also unto thee, that thou art Peter, and upon this rock I will build my church..."

- The Bible refers to what Peter knew and how Peter knew it, is going to be the structure of how God will communicate and build His Church. To build mean to give structure. A building is made with the purpose of being inhabited with protection. Remember "Church" means "Called Out". The status and judgements that God blesses us through or we can say, the structure and system that God has built for us to live and operate our lives, is to know that "Jesus the Anointed One" with the power to remove burdens and destroy yokes is on top of the hill for us. He is making intercession just like Moses. We have full access to Him and know that we must do our part by having faith.

  - We shall win the battle.
  - We must carry out the instructions suggested by our faith sense and put all other suggestions from all our other senses under the control of our faith sense.

"...and the gates of hell shall not prevail against it."

- This tells us that that we are fighting against spiritual forces. It also tells us that the strategies used by those spiritual forces will not prevail (win) against the system and methods that we are using as a "Holy

Nation." If we use what we have learnt in this book we will always win. We will always overcome. We will always prosper and we will always be blessed.

Here is what we should be doing at the bottom of the hill.

Matthew 16:19
"And I will give unto thee the keys of the kingdom of heaven: and whatsoever thou shalt bind on earth shall be bound in heaven: and whatsoever thou shalt loose on earth shall be loosed in heaven."

Our training and what we have learnt is what is known as "the key to the kingdom". Our fighting is to take what we know and use it to bind. The best way I can describe the meaning of the word "Bind" in this context is;
- ☐ To speak with confidence because of what we know.
- ☐ To stop, refrain and limit an opponent from succeeding.

We must also note that the same result will happen in the heaven.

The second part to our fighting is to loose on earth. The best way I can describe the meaning of the word "Loose" in this context is;
- ☐ To untie, to free, to loosen or to remove.

Philippians 2:10-11
"That at the name of Jesus every knee should bow, of things
in heaven, and things in earth, and things under the earth;
And that every tongue should confess that Jesus Christ is
Lord, to the glory of God the Father."

The whole topic was based on who Jesus is. He is the Christ.
That's why He is known as "Jesus Christ" or "Jesus the Christ"
which means "Jesus the Anointed One" which means "Jesus
the Burden Remover and The Yoke Destroyer".

Isaiah 10:27
"And it shall come to pass in that day, that his burden shall
be taken away from off thy shoulder, and his yoke from off
thy neck, and the yoke shall be destroyed because of the
anointing."

The burdens are lifted off our shoulder and the yoke loosed
and taken off our neck by the anointing power that we now
have access by doing what we have learnt in this book
and also how we have been trained as part of God's Nation.
We have access to the top of the hill whilst we are doing our
fighting at the bottom of the hill. What we "bind" here
will be "bind" in spiritual places and what we "loose" here
will be "loose" in spiritual places.

Mark 16:17-20

"And these signs shall follow them that believe; In my name shall they cast out devils; they shall speak with new tongues; They shall take up serpents; and if they drink any deadly thing, it shall not hurt them; they shall lay hands on the sick, and they shall recover. So then after the Lord had spoken unto them, he was received up into heaven, and sat on the right hand of God. And they went forth, and preached everywhere, the Lord working with them, and confirming the word with signs following. Amen."

Jesus has the authority to do this and is doing this today through us.

Ephesians 1:22-23

"And hath put all things under his feet, and gave him to be the head over all things to the church, Which is his body, the fullness of him that filleth all in all."

This is why He requires a Holy Nation. This is why He requires us. The verse above tells us that He is the head of all things to the church which is His body. The church, us, God's called out ones, are not only His Holy Nation, we are also His Body. God through the Name of Jesus Christ is still casting out devils, speaking to people all over the world using different languages, protecting us in dangerous environment and from life threatening things, providing healing for the sick and seeing them recover and what is so amazing is that because we are His body, He is doing it through us. He is using us. He is protecting us. God is working with us and confirming the word with signs and wonders following. We are the fullness of Him that filleth all in all. We are His Holy Nation fighting the good fight of faith and winning, and then we become a witness to other nations in the world today. We are the ones who will prove God and be seen as a wise and understanding people. We will be seen as a "Great Nation".

Psalms 103:19
"The Lord hath prepared his throne in the heavens; and his kingdom ruleth over all."

Jesus' throne has been prepared in the heavens and His kingdom rule over all. His status and judgement rule over all. His structure, presence and protection rule over all. When we do what is required of us, God will command the blessing that will give us victory and when we apply the principles of this book we will have victory over the Amalekites in our lives.

Hebrews 11:6

"But without faith it is impossible to please him: for he that cometh to God must believe that he is, and that he is a rewarder of them that diligently seek him."

Through having church at home we are doing what is known as "diligently seeking him". God will reward ALL that "diligently seek him".

Exodus 17:11-16

"And it came to pass, when Moses held up his hand, that Israel prevailed: and when he let down his hand, Amalek prevailed. But Moses' hands were heavy; and they took a stone, and put it under him, and he sat thereon; and Aaron and Hur stayed up his hands, the one on the one side, and the other on the other side; and his hands were steady until the going down of the sun. And Joshua discomfited Amalek and his people with the edge of the sword. And the Lord said unto Moses, Write this for a memorial in a book, and rehearse it in the ears of Joshua: for I will utterly put out the remembrance of Amalek from under heaven. And Moses built an altar, and called the name of it Jehovah–nissi: For he said, Because the Lord hath sworn that the Lord will have war with Amalek from generation to generation."

When we are under a banner that banner represents all that we stand for. It stands for and states that we are under the protection, support, laws and government of that banner. We are under the banner of the Lord and it should be spiritually waved in front of the Amalekites in our lives at battle. If we believe and follow the instructions of this book we will win and be victorious.

Romans 8:31
"What shall we then say to these things? If God be for us, who can be against us?"

In this current time and environment, God is visiting us at home. He is looking for families that should be ready to fight as part of His "Holy Nation". He is looking for people to be a part of his body so He can do good for them and heal people that are oppressed by the devil.

Today is the time to obey our calling. To start or continue our training.

Are you a part of His family or are you a part of His Nation?

- ☐ If you are of the family mentality, get some training to become part of His "Holy Nation".

- ☐ If you are of the "Holy Nation" mentality, use your training to fight and overcome the Amalekites in your lives.

Joshua 24:15
"...but as for me and my house, we will serve the LORD."

As for me and my house, we shall obey the Lord. We will serve the Lord with our hearts. We will be a part of His 'Holy Nation'. We are ready to be used by His Holy Spirit to do good, heal others and free those that are oppressed by the devil. We will fight the good fight of faith and win having victory over all our enemies. We shall be a witness to others that we belong to a wise and understanding set of people. A Holy Nation chosen by God.

The Word of God tells us that God thinks from generation to generation. A vision will always pass through generations within a family. The mantel, or the gift or that special anointing is passed from generation to generation until its purpose is fulfilled. That purpose and vision will pass through the family tree. When we apply what we have learnt from this book, we will be of the understanding that, from a family, to a nation, to a family tree.

Psalms 1
He shall be like a tree (family tree) planted by the rivers of water (nourished and on good ground) that bring forth it's fruit in its season (bring forth fruit at the right timing) and whatever he does shall prosper (not fail, be successful, be fruitful and God perfect will.)

This is what God wants for your family, your branches, your leaves, and for your offspring. To bring forth fruit in its season and whatever, those in your family do, it shall prosper in the end.

It all starts with the title of this book...
"As For Me And My House..."

I pray that you will continue to grow daily in your romantic relationship with God and this book has been a blessing to you.

In Jesus Name.
Amen.

Printed in Great Britain
by Amazon

29804115R00053

CHAPTER 6

Extended Love

From the last chapter we have understood the following;

"Everything about Me is three dimensional"
"Everything about you is three dimensional"
"Our relationship is three dimensional"

When God spoke to me about three dimensional this is what
He was trying to tell me.

"Everything about Me is extended love"
"Everything about you is extended love"
"Our relationship is extended love"

The word "Extension" means "To increase or enlarge
something".

I remember when a friend of mine was buying a house and
he wanted my opinion to see if there was a spiritual
agreement with his intended purchase. This friend was an
architect by trade, so he understood the qualities and
potential possibilities, also what he should look for when
purchasing a property. On the way to view the house he
was going to purchase we stopped and looked at two other
houses next door to each other. He said "Ricky
look at this house. This is a nice house. What do you
think?" I looked at the house and thought it was a nice
house with a garage attached on the side. It looked like a

three bedroom house with a nice driveway at the front. I answered "It's alright I suppose." With excitement in his eyes he then said "Now look at next door." When I look at next door the house looked much bigger, better and nicer than the house we were focusing on before. I instantly said "Now this is a quality house that I would like for you to be blessed with. I myself would like to be blessed with a house like this. This house has character." He turned and looked at the first house and said "Ricky this house is a very good purchase for the price and has great potential. Being a man of faith I began to get a little frustrated that he was looking at the lesser when the greater was in front of our eyes. I said "Stop looking at that house! You can afford a house like this bigger one. I don't want to discuss anything more about that smaller house anymore. Then he said "Ricky look at them both closely. They are both the same. The only difference is that the people who own the house that you like have built an extension where the garage was and cleaned up their drive and added a nice gate. I heard his words and looked closely. To my amazement he was correct. The houses were both of identical structure and the main difference which made that house so beautiful was the extension. I then looked at him and said "What a big difference an extension can make when it is done properly." He then said, "The house I am purchasing is like the house without the extension and I will be saving a lot of money. When I purchase it I will build an extension just like this one and it will increase a lot in value and look beautiful as the house that you like.